I0427437

CUSTOMER RETENTION TECHNIQUES

Increasing client loyalty & reducing churn All the details you need to grasp & master sales, with tried-and-true methods to boost sales, satisfaction, & impose your will

RICHARD N. WILLIAMS

All right reserved. No part of this publication may be reproduced, distributed or transmitted in any form or by any means including photocopy, recording or other electronic or mechanical methods, without the prior written permission of the publisher, except in the case of brief quotations embodied in critical reviews and

certain other noncommercial uses permitted by copyright law.
Copyright Richard N. Williams

TABLE OF CONTENTS

INTRODUCT ION

Chloe found herself in charge of a struggling tech company in the bustling heart of Silicon Valley, where innovation echoed through every startup. The test was stupendous: their client degrees of consistency were falling, and the murmurs of beat repeated stronger than the murmur of servers in their office.

Chloe, a carefully prepared business person with a strong soul, realized that a change was fundamental as well as basic for the endurance of the organization. She gathered her team, a diverse group of talented people, and set out to rethink their approach to keeping customers.

The initial step was understanding the trouble spots. Chloe prompted a progression of inside and out interviews with existing clients. As the tales unfurled, designs arose - correspondence holes, neglected assumptions, and an absence of customized commitment. It was a sobering second, yet one that energized the group's assurance to enhance.

Equipped with experiences, they set off on a mission to redo their client support procedure. Rather than depending entirely on robotized reactions, they executed a more human touch. Each client inquiry got a customized answer, and the group focused on proactively resolving possible issues before they heightened. The outcomes were amazing - besides the fact that fulfillment appraised rise, however clients felt appreciated and esteemed.

Embracing innovation as a partner, the group presented a client reliability application. This application followed buys as well as accumulated information on client inclinations and conduct. Outfitted with this data, the organization could now fit their administrations to address individual issues. It was a little, at this point critical, move toward building enduring connections.

To additionally cement client devotion, Chloe acquainted a gamification component with the application. Clients acquired focuses for buys as well as for drawing in with the brand via online entertainment, alluding companions, and giving criticism. The prizes were cautiously organized - elite admittance to new elements, customized limits, and, surprisingly, an opportunity to go to organization occasions. Customers gained a sense of belonging as a result of the gamification strategy, which transformed routine transactions into an engaging experience.

In the always advancing scene of tech, remaining on the ball was fundamental. Chloe urged her group to go to industry meetings, to grandstand their items as well as to effectively draw in with clients eye to eye. These interactions were more than just business deals. They gave the team a chance to learn about their clients' changing needs and show how much they loved what they did.

A buzz of excitement surrounded the brand as word of the company's customer-centric approach spread. It wasn't just about the item any longer; it was tied in with being essential for a local area that minded. Chloe understood that the tale of their change was just about as imperative as the mechanical progressions they were making.

Chloe was in charge of a storytelling campaign that aimed to immortalize this journey and inspire the team as well as their customers. They produced video testimonials in which long-term customers discuss their experiences, including the difficulties they encountered, the response they received, and the development of their partnership. Their brand identity was built on these stories, which were shared on social media and used in marketing campaigns.

As the change unfurled, Chloe realized that flexibility was vital. Economic downturns, unanticipated shifts in the market, and even a global pandemic all presented challenges. However, the organization endured these hardships by remaining consistent with their obligation to consumer loyalty. They carried out exceptional drives, offering expanded help during difficult stretches, and went above and beyond to guarantee their clients felt upheld.

The outcomes were reflected in their monetary records as well as in the certified tributes from clients who had become advocates. The organization that was once near the precarious edge of lack of clarity was presently a reference point of development, strength, and client devotion.

Chloe's process instructed her that client maintenance wasn't simply a business system - it was a demonstration of the force of human association. In the domain of tech, where calculations and codes frequently ruled discussions, she had demonstrated that compassion, personalization, and a veritable obligation to client achievement were the genuine drivers of enduring change.

Overview of Customer Retention

A company's efforts and initiatives to retain its existing customer base comprise customer retention, which is a crucial component of any business strategy. In a profoundly serious market, where client procurement expenses can be critical, holding faithful clients becomes central for practical achievement. The most important aspects, advantages, and strategies of customer retention will be discussed in depth in this overview.

Significance of Client Maintenance

Cost-Viability: Obtaining new clients can be multiple times more costly than holding existing ones. Client maintenance methodologies expect to expand the worth obtained from current clients, lessening the requirement for consistent securing endeavors.

Income Steadiness: Existing clients are bound to make rehash buys, adding to a steady income stream. Long haul client connections frequently bring about higher lifetime client esteem, which is the all out income a client produces over their whole relationship with the organization.

Brand Promotion: Fulfilled clients are probably going to remain as well as become brand advocates. They can assume a significant part in verbal exchange promoting, impacting others to pick the organization's items or administrations.

Customer Experience (CX) components of customer retention: A positive client experience is central to maintenance. It covers everything a customer does when they interact with the brand, from looking at the website to getting help. Personalization, comfort, and powerful correspondence add to a consistent client venture.

Client support: Extraordinary client care is a foundation of client maintenance. Convenient and powerful goals of issues or requests can transform a possibly regrettable encounter into a positive one, reinforcing the client's association with the brand.

Dedication Projects: Offering motivators, limits, or restrictive admittance to steadfast clients supports rehash business. Dedication programs make a feeling of having a place and prize clients for their proceeds with support.

Correspondence Techniques: Normal, customized correspondence keeps an association with clients. This can incorporate bulletins, designated advancements, or updates on new items and administrations. Engaging and retaining customers comes from keeping them informed.

Advantages of Client Maintenance

Expanded Client Lifetime Worth (CLV): Client maintenance straightforwardly influences CLV. By expanding the span of the client brand relationship and empowering rehash buys, the general worth a client brings to the business is improved.

Reduced Rates of Churn: Beat, or the rate at which clients quit working with an organization, is a key measurement in client maintenance. Fruitful maintenance methodologies lead to bringing down stir rates, demonstrating a better, more steady client base.

Positive Standing: Fulfilled clients are probably going to share their positive encounters, adding to a positive brand notoriety. This can draw in new clients and further set the steadfastness of existing ones.

Upper hand: In a market where items and administrations can be comparable, remarkable client maintenance can be a special selling recommendation. Companies gain a competitive advantage over their rivals when they prioritize and excel in customer retention.

Client Maintenance Methodologies

Personalization: A sense of uniqueness is created when products, services, and communication are tailored to individual customer preferences. Personalization can be accomplished through information investigation, figuring out client conduct, and utilizing innovation.

Input and Studies: Consistently looking for input from clients gives significant experiences into their fulfillment levels and regions for development. Carrying out changes in view of this criticism shows clients that their perspectives matter.

Predictable Quality: Consistency in item or administration quality is vital for client maintenance. Meeting or surpassing client assumptions fabricates trust and trust in the brand.

Problem Solving Ahead of Time: Distinguishing and resolving issues before they raise exhibits a promise to consumer loyalty. Proactive issue goals include observing client criticism, expecting possible issues, and making a quick move.

Measurements for Client Maintenance Estimation

Client Degree of consistency (CRR): The percentage of customers who remain clients over a given time frame is the basis for this metric. It is determined by taking away the quantity of new clients obtained from the all out clients toward the start of the period and separating the outcome by the underlying number of clients.

Agitate Rate: The beat rate addresses the level of clients who quit utilizing an item or administration throughout a given time. Better customer retention is indicated by a lower churn rate.

Net Advertiser Score (NPS): NPS estimates the probability of clients prescribing an organization's items or

8

administrations to other people. Clients are sorted as advertisers, passives, or naysayers, giving bits of knowledge into general fulfillment.

Client Lifetime Worth (CLV): CLV evaluates the complete income a client is supposed to produce all through their relationship with the organization. A higher CLV implies more grounded client maintenance.

All in all, client maintenance is a diverse procedure enveloping different components pointed toward safeguarding and improving the connection between an organization and its clients. Focusing on consumer loyalty, utilizing powerful correspondence, and carrying out designated maintenance systems add to a reasonable and prosperous plan of action. As organizations keep on exploring a powerful commercial center, understanding and putting resources into client maintenance will stay a foundation of long haul achievement.

Importance of Building Customer Loyalty

Building client dedication is principal for the supported achievement and development of any business. In an undeniably cutthroat market, where buyers are barraged with decisions, cultivating a steadfast client base can be a unique advantage. Loyalty extends beyond transactional relationships; it makes a drawn out connection between the client and the brand. The significance of building client reliability couldn't possibly be more significant, as it straightforwardly influences an organization's income, image picture, and generally maintainability.

One of the essential benefits of client faithfulness is its immediate relationship with income development. Faithful clients will more often than not make rehashed buys, contributing fundamentally to a business' primary concern. The expense of securing another client is regularly higher than holding a current one, making client dependability a savvy system. At the point when clients are faithful to a brand, they are bound to pick its items or administrations over contenders, regardless of whether the costs are somewhat higher. This reliable stream of income from rehash business gives dependability and permits organizations to put resources into development and extension.

Besides, faithful clients can become brand advocates, assuming a significant part in drawing in new clients. Fulfilled clients are bound to prescribe a brand to their companions, family, and partners. Positive reviews can significantly increase a brand's visibility and credibility in today's interconnected world, where word-of-mouth spreads quickly through social media and online reviews. This natural development driven by steadfast clients makes a positive input circle, where fulfilled clients draw in new ones, further upgrading the organization's market presence.

Past monetary advantages, client reliability adds to a positive brand picture. Organizations that focus on consumer loyalty and construct enduring connections are seen as dependable and solid. This positive discernment reinforces the bond with existing clients as well as draws in new ones who are looking for a brand they can trust. A positive brand picture is a strong resource in the present cutthroat scene, where shoppers are buying items as well as conforming to brands that mirror their qualities and inclinations.

Client steadfastness is intently attached to client experience. Organizations that put resources into giving an outstanding client experience make a profound association with their clients. A positive customer experience encourages loyalty through personalized services, effective problem solving, or engaging interactions. Clients are bound to stay faithful to a brand that reliably meets or surpasses their assumptions. Conversely, an unfortunate client experience can prompt disappointment and brief clients to investigate choices, gambling with the deficiency of significant connections.

Besides, building client steadfastness is a continuous cycle that requires proactive commitment. Customary correspondence with clients, customized offers, and steadfastness programs are powerful apparatuses to fortify the relationship. Steadfastness programs, specifically, give substantial compensations to client reliability, empowering rehash business. These projects can incorporate limits, selective admittance to items or administrations, or even a focused framework that collects with each purchase. Such impetuses improve client maintenance as well as make a feeling of appreciation and worth, cultivating a good close to home association.

In the present information driven time, organizations approach immense measures of client data. Using this information actually can essentially add to building client faithfulness. Figuring out client inclinations, buy history, and input permits organizations to tailor their contributions and correspondence systems. Personalization, whether in advertising efforts or item proposals, exhibits to clients that their singular requirements are recognized and esteemed. This degree of personalization goes quite far in building areas of strength for an association, which is a vital driver of faithfulness.

All in all, the significance of building client faithfulness couldn't possibly be more significant in the dynamic and cutthroat business climate. Loyal customers contribute to brand advocacy, a positive brand image, and sustained growth in addition to the immediate financial benefits. Organizations that focus on consumer loyalty, put resources into making outstanding client encounters, and influence information to customize communications are better situated to fabricate enduring connections. In a time where shoppers have bountiful options, client reliability is the foundation of progress, giving a strong groundwork to organizations to flourish and thrive.

Understanding Churn in Business

In the context of business, churn is the rate at which customers stop using a product or service over a certain amount of time. Understanding beat is vital for organizations as it straightforwardly influences income and development. This peculiarity isn't restricted to a specific industry; rather, a general concern requests cautious examination and vital reaction.

The most important phase in fathoming agitation is to perceive its two essential sorts: intentional and compulsory. When customers decide to stop using a product or service for a variety of reasons, this is called voluntary churn. This can come from disappointment, better choices on the lookout, or evolving needs. In contrast, involuntary churn is caused by external factors like economic downturns, company closures, or unanticipated customer events.

Estimating stir is a crucial part of figuring out its suggestions. The beat rate is normally communicated as a rate and is determined by partitioning the quantity of clients lost during a particular period by the complete number of clients toward the start of that period. This measurement gives an unmistakable image of how well a business is holding its client base.

Distinguishing the underlying drivers of beat is fundamental for contriving successful maintenance techniques. Data analytics, surveys, and feedback from customers can provide insight into the reasons why customers are leaving. Normal elements adding to intentional stir incorporate unfortunate item quality, deficient client assistance, or serious estimating somewhere else. Compulsory agitate might be connected to monetary variables or disturbances in help.

Maintenance endeavors ought to be customized to address the particular explanations for client stir. Further developing item quality, upgrading client support, and remaining cutthroat in valuing are normal systems for decreasing willful stir. For compulsory beat, organizations might have to zero in on making adaptable installment plans, offering limits during monetary slumps, or broadening item contributions to adjust to changing economic situations.

Understanding churn patterns is made easier with the help of customer segmentation. Not all clients are similar, and their explanations behind beating might differ. By classifying clients in view of socio economics, conduct, or use designs, organizations can recognize high-risk sections and carry out designated maintenance techniques. For example, a section with a high centralization of cost delicate clients could profit from exceptional limits or faithfulness programs.

Prescient examination is one more amazing asset in the fight against agitation. By utilizing verifiable information and AI calculations, organizations can conjecture which clients are probably going to stir from now on. This proactive methodology empowers organizations to intercede before clients choose to leave, expanding the viability of maintenance endeavors.

The client venture assumes a critical part in understanding and fighting beat. From the underlying contact to post-buy communications, each touchpoint adds to the general client experience. Investigating the client venture recognizes trouble spots and regions for development, permitting organizations to improve fulfillment and faithfulness.

Openness is absolutely vital in decreasing beat. Consistently captivating with clients through designated correspondence, like bulletins, refreshes, or customized offers, keeps an association and keeps the brand top-of-mind. Besides, laying out a criticism circle urges clients to voice concerns and furnishes organizations with significant data to instantly resolve issues.

In a membership based plan of action, client maintenance is principal. Offering added esteem through ceaseless improvement, selective substance, or customized encounters can altogether affect consumer loyalty and diminish stir. Also, giving simple retraction choices and straightforward charging rehearses cultivates trust and positive client connections.

Worker fulfillment and commitment likewise assume a part in grasping the beat. A propelled and thoroughly prepared group is bound to convey outstanding client care, emphatically impacting client maintenance. To boost employee morale, businesses should make investments in ongoing training programs, employee recognition, and the creation of a positive work environment.

Understanding the larger market landscape necessitates a thorough understanding of competitors. It is possible to gain useful insights by keeping an eye on the offerings, pricing strategies, and levels of customer satisfaction of competitors. Businesses can identify opportunities for innovation and improvement in order to remain competitive in the market by staying up to date on industry trends and benchmarking themselves against rivals.

Understanding the beat isn't just about recognizing the deficiency of clients; it's tied in with digging into the purposes for it and proactively carrying out techniques to moderate it. Organizations that focus on client maintenance, utilize information driven bits of knowledge, and cultivate positive client encounters are better situated to flourish in a cutthroat market. As the business scene develops, adjusting to changing client needs and inclinations becomes principal in building a versatile and fruitful undertaking.

Chapter 1
Key Factors Influencing Customer Retention

Client maintenance is a basic part of any business' prosperity, impacted by different key factors that organizations should comprehend and address in a calculated way. These variables assume a vital part in molding client dedication and deciding if purchasers will keep on disparaging a brand or look for options. By digging into these key powerhouses, organizations can foster viable maintenance methodologies to encourage long haul client connections.

Client Experience:

One of the essential variables impacting client maintenance is the general experience a client has with a brand. Every touchpoint a customer has with a business influences their perception. A consistent, positive experience creates a feeling of fulfillment and reliability. Going against the norm, unfortunate encounters, whether through client assistance, item quality, or ease of use, can prompt disappointment and drive clients away. Organizations that focus on conveying uncommon client encounters are bound to hold their customers.

Client support:

The nature of client care is a vital determinant in client maintenance. Expeditious and supportive reactions to questions, productive issue goal, and customized collaborations add to positive client encounters. A responsive and sympathetic client support group fabricates trust and builds up a client's obligation to a brand. Alternatively, unfortunate client care can bring about dissatisfaction and push clients to investigate options, influencing maintenance adversely.

Innovation and quality of the product:

The center contribution of a business, its items or administrations, essentially impacts client maintenance. Loyalty is built by consistently providing high-quality goods that meet or exceed customer expectations. Moreover, organizations that constantly develop and refresh their contributions to address advancing client needs and market patterns are better situated to hold their client base. Stagnation in item improvement might lead clients to look for additional creative arrangements somewhere else.

An incentive for Cash:

Clients look for an incentive for the cash they put resources into an item or administration. Promotions and loyalty programs have the potential to enhance the perceived value proposition, so pricing should align with perceived value. Customer satisfaction and loyalty can be bolstered by providing options that are both affordable and of high quality, as well as by occasionally offering special deals or discounts. Alternatively, evaluating methodologies that appear to be unreasonable or neglect to legitimize the item's worth might drive clients away.

Correspondence and Commitment:

Customers are more likely to stick with a brand if you communicate with them on a consistent basis and in a meaningful way. Connecting with clients through customized correspondences, like bulletins, updates, and extraordinary offers, keeps the brand top-of-mind. Businesses can respond to feedback and interact with their audience through interactive communication on social media platforms. An absence of correspondence or forgetting to address client concerns can prompt a decrease in consistency standards.

Brand Notoriety:

The standing of a brand fundamentally impacts client maintenance. Positive surveys, tributes, and a solid web-based presence add to a good insight. On the other hand, negative surveys or a discolored standing can disintegrate trust and drive clients away. To ensure that their brand image reflects the values and expectations of their target audience, businesses must actively manage and enhance it.

Client Input and Versatility:

Focusing on client input is essential for figuring out their requirements and concerns. Organizations that effectively look for and use client input show a promise to progress. Being versatile and receptive to changing client inclinations guarantees that a brand stays important. Inability to develop with client assumptions might bring about diminished maintenance as clients move to contenders who better meet their advancing requirements.

Accessibility and Convenience:

Customers value accessibility and ease of use in this fast-paced world. Customers are more likely to stay with a company if it has user-friendly websites, simple purchasing procedures, and hassle-free customer support. This reaches out to factors like adaptable installment choices, ideal conveyances, and advantageous merchandise exchanges. Any grating in these cycles can prompt disappointment and adversely influence maintenance.

Profound Association:

Building a close to home association with clients goes past conditional connections. Brands that summon positive feelings, line up with client esteems, and make important encounters lay out a more profound association. Profound bonds improve client reliability, making it more probable that clients will keep on picking a specific brand over contenders, in any event, when confronted with comparative contributions.

Serious Scene:

The serious climate assumes a vital part in client maintenance. Organizations should know about contenders' methodologies, valuing, and contributions to guarantee they stay serious. Offering distinct value propositions can help a brand stand out and increase customer loyalty. Overlooking or misjudging the serious scene might bring about clients being tricked away by additional engaging other options.

client maintenance is a multi-layered try that requires a comprehensive methodology. By getting it and tending to these key elements, organizations can develop areas of strength, associations with their clients, cultivating dependability and adding to long haul achievement. A consistent commitment to providing value, adapting to shifting customer dynamics, and creating positive brand experiences are all necessary components of effective retention strategies.

Quality of Products/Services

Nature of items and administrations assumes a critical part in client maintenance procedures for organizations. In a cutthroat market where decisions proliferate, holding clients is basically as urgent as securing new ones. A critical determinant in this try is the steady conveyance of excellent items and administrations. Let's examine the significance of quality and the ways in which it aids in effective customer retention.

Above all else, quality lays out trust. At the point when clients get items or administrations that reliably meet or surpass their assumptions, it constructs a feeling of trust and unwavering quality. Trust is the groundwork of any fruitful long haul relationship, and in the domain of business, this relationship is between the client and the organization. At the point when clients believe that a business will reliably give quality, they are bound to stay faithful.

Moreover, quality items and administrations contribute altogether to consumer loyalty. Fulfilled clients are bound to become recurrent clients, and their positive encounters can prompt verbal exchange references, which are strong in drawing in new clients. In the present interconnected world, fulfilled clients can immediately become brand diplomats through virtual entertainment and online surveys, enhancing the effect of value on client maintenance.

Furthermore, great contributions add to client devotion. Customers are less likely to look into other options when they find goods or services that consistently satisfy their requirements and offer value. Steadfastness goes past simple fulfillment; it suggests a responsibility and close to home association with a brand. Building such dependability requires a supported spotlight on conveying greatness in each connection.

Quality likewise straightforwardly impacts the apparent worth of an item or administration. For products they believe to be of high quality, customers are willing to pay a premium. This eagerness to pay something else for quality isn't just about the unmistakable parts of an item; it stretches out to the general client experience, including administration, backing, and post-buy commitment. Organizations that focus on quality can frequently order greater costs, which, thus, can decidedly influence income and benefit.

In the period of virtual entertainment and online surveys, one negative experience can rapidly discolor a brand's standing. Quality goes about as a safeguard against negative criticism. A business reliably conveying top notch items and administrations is better prepared to climate incidental misfortunes. Besides, when issues do emerge, a standing for quality can mellow the effect, as clients are bound to assume the best about a brand they trust.

Customer retention is about more than just the first purchase; it's tied in with cultivating a continuous relationship. Quality items and administrations add to this relationship by making a positive client experience at each touchpoint. Whether it's the convenience of an item, the responsiveness of client service, or the sturdiness of the thing, every perspective adds to the general client experience. Organizations that focus on quality in each part of their tasks are better situated to make enduring associations with their clients.

Conversely, an absence of value can prompt disappointment and, eventually, client stir. On the off chance that an item reliably neglects to measure up to assumptions, or on the other hand assuming that client care is deficient in responsiveness and viability, clients are probably going to look for choices. The expense of obtaining another client is in many cases a lot higher than holding a current one, making client maintenance through quality a practical system for organizations.

Quality likewise assumes an urgent part in client criticism and improvement. Organizations that esteem quality are bound to effectively look for and use client criticism to persistently upgrade their items and administrations. This iterative course of progress helps in holding existing clients as well as positions the business as versatile and client driven, drawing in new clients who focus on quality in their buying choices.

All in all, the nature of items and administrations is a foundation of compelling client maintenance methods. It assembles trust, cultivates fulfillment and steadfastness, upgrades apparent worth, shields notoriety, and adds to a general positive client experience. In a serious market, organizations that focus on and reliably convey quality are better situated to hold clients, drive client devotion, and flourish over the long haul. Quality isn't simply an element; a pledge to greatness delivers profits in client maintenance and supported business achievement.

Customer Experience and Communication Strategies

Client Experience (CX) and compelling correspondence systems are vital parts of any effective business. Companies are aware that providing an exceptional customer experience is not only a differentiator but also a requirement for long-term growth in today's dynamic and competitive market. This article delves into key principles and practices that can improve a brand's relationship with its customers and examines the crucial relationship between customer experience and communication strategies.

Understanding Client Experience:

Client Experience envelopes each collaboration a client has with a brand, from starting attention to post-buy support. It encompasses the entire customer journey and emotional connection, transcending the product or service itself. Positive client encounters fabricate reliability, drive rehash business, and produce positive verbal exchange advertising.

Comprehensive Excursion Planning:

Making a consistent client venture includes understanding touchpoints across different channels. Planning the client's whole communication recognizes trouble spots and regions for development. Whether it's a site visit, web-based entertainment cooperation, or in-store insight, each touchpoint adds to the general discernment.

Personalization:

Fitting encounters to individual inclinations improves consumer loyalty. Utilizing information to comprehend client conduct permits organizations to present customized suggestions, limits, or content. This further develops consumer loyalty as well as fortifies the brand-client relationship.

The Function of Communication Techniques:

Powerful correspondence is the bedrock of a positive client experience. How a brand conveys, both inside and remotely, essentially impacts client insight.

Consistent voice for the brand:

Keeping a predictable brand voice across all correspondence diverts helps in building a conspicuous character. Whether through promoting materials, client care corporations, or web-based entertainment posts, a brought together voice cultivates brand trust and steadfastness.

Clear and Straightforward Informing:

Lucidity and straightforwardness in correspondence are foremost. Clients value genuineness about item highlights, evaluating, and approaches. Open communication and prompt resolution of problems foster trust and credibility.

Mix of CX and Correspondence Systems:

Input Circles:

Companies can gain insights directly from customers by establishing robust feedback mechanisms. Investigating this input gives important data to refine correspondence systems and upgrade the general client experience.

Omnichannel Correspondence:

In the present interconnected world, clients draw in with brands through different channels. A powerful correspondence procedure incorporates these channels consistently. A coordinated strategy ensures that the brand's message remains consistent across all channels, including social media, email, and in-person interactions.

Technology for Better Customer Experience:

Chatbots and AI:

Incorporating man-made reasoning (computer based intelligence) and chatbots smoothes out client associations. Mechanized reactions can deal with routine questions, opening up HR to resolve more mind boggling issues. This further develops proficiency as well as guarantees day in and day out accessibility.

Information Examination:

Tackling the force of information investigation gives significant bits of knowledge into client conduct. By understanding inclinations and trouble spots, organizations can fit correspondence systems to address explicit client needs.

Worker Preparing and Strengthening:
Client Driven Culture:

Encouraging a client driven culture inside the association is urgent. Employees are more likely to act in this way in their interactions when they are aware of the significance of providing positive customer experiences. Ceaseless preparation supports the meaning of superb client care.

Enabling Forefront Staff:

Most of the time, frontline workers are the company's face. Enabling them to simply decide and determine issues speedily upgrades the general client experience. This requires giving sufficient preparation and assets to actually deal with different situations.

Contextual analyses:

Amazon - Personalization and Proficient Correspondence:

Amazon's prosperity is mostly ascribed to its customized proposals in light of client perusing and buying history. The consistent correspondence across its foundation, from request affirmation messages to constant following updates, epitomizes successful correspondence techniques.

Apple - Predictable Brand Insight:

Apple's obligation to a predictable brand experience is obvious in its smooth item plans, moderate showcasing, and easy to use interfaces. This consistency reverberates through each correspondence, supporting the brand's personality and encouraging client dependability.

Difficulties and Future Patterns:

Information Security Concerns:

Personalization and privacy must be balanced. Clients are turning out to be more mindful of information protection issues, and organizations should explore this scene cautiously. To maintain trust, open communication regarding data usage is essential.

Ascent of Visual and Voice Correspondence:

With the rising utilization of visuals and voice connections, brands need to adjust their correspondence methodologies. Consolidating sight and sound components in showcasing materials and embracing voice-actuated advancements guarantees pertinence in developing shopper inclinations.

The cooperative energy between client experience and correspondence techniques is urgent for organizations endeavoring to flourish in a cutthroat market. By understanding the all encompassing client venture, carrying out successful correspondence practices, and utilizing innovation, organizations can make significant encounters that reverberate with their crowd. Putting resources into a client driven culture and remaining sensitive to arising patterns will situate organizations to meet as well as surpass client assumptions, encouraging long haul connections and practical achievement.

Pricing and Value Proposition

Client maintenance is a basic part of any business system, and a powerful methodology includes a cautious thought of evaluating and a convincing incentive. The transaction between these components assumes a vital part in holding clients and encouraging long haul connections.

Pricing Strategies for Keeping Customers:

Divided Evaluating:

Utilizing divided valuing is a viable method for holding different client gatherings. Fitting estimating plans in view of client sections permits organizations to take special care of various necessities and spending plans. For example, offering layered membership plans with fluctuating degrees of highlights or administrations guarantees that clients can track down a reasonable choice, advancing reliability.

Limits and Motivating forces:

Giving limits or motivating forces to steadfast clients urges them to remain focused on a brand. This could incorporate reliability programs, selective limits, or early admittance to new items. Businesses not only retain customers but also foster a positive brand image by rewarding loyalty.

Pricing that Changes:

Carrying out powerful evaluating includes changing costs in view of market interest, contender estimating, or client conduct. This system empowers organizations to stay cutthroat and receptive to advertise changes, consequently holding clients who are delicate to valuing variances.

Packaging Administrations:

Packaging administrations or items at a limited rate can be a strong maintenance method. This approach not just adds an incentive for clients by giving a practical bundle yet in addition makes it easier for them to change to contenders offering comparative independent items.

Offer in Client Maintenance:

Personalization:

Creating a customized incentive includes understanding and meeting individual client needs. By using client information, organizations can tailor their contributions, correspondences, and encounters, making a one of a kind incentive that reverberates with every client.

Extraordinary Client support:

An exceptional client care experience is a critical driver of maintenance. Answering instantly to requests, settling issues effectively, and going above and beyond to guarantee consumer loyalty contribute fundamentally to the apparent worth clients get from a brand.

Persistent Development:

A guarantee to development guarantees that an organization's items or administrations stay important and serious. Consistently presenting new highlights, updates, or upgrades shows a commitment to meeting developing client needs, supporting the offer.

Straightforwardness and Trust:

Building trust through straightforwardness is pivotal for client maintenance. A sense of reliability is established when pricing structures, terms, and policies are clearly communicated, reducing customers' levels of uncertainty and fostering trusting relationships over time.

Instructive Substance:

Giving significant substance that teaches and helps clients in expanding the advantages of an item or administration improves the general offer. Tutorials, guides, and webinars that give customers more power and make them more engaged with the brand are examples of this.

Combination of Evaluating and Incentive:

Alignment of the Strategy:

Guaranteeing arrangement among estimating and the incentive is fundamental. The apparent worth of an item or administration ought to legitimize its cost, making an agreeable relationship. Clients are bound to remain steadfast when they accept they are getting fair incentive for the cash they contribute.

Feedback Systems:

Laying out input instruments empowers organizations to comprehend client view of both estimating and the incentive. Investigating client criticism gives significant experiences to calibrating estimating systems and refining the offer to all the more likely to meet client assumptions.

Information Driven Independent direction:

Utilizing information examination helps in going with informed choices in regards to estimating changes and offering upgrades. By investigating client conduct, inclinations, and market patterns, organizations can adjust their methodologies to amplify client maintenance.

Techniques for Interaction:

Really conveying changes in evaluating or offering changes is pivotal. Straightforwardness in these correspondences constructs trust and permits clients to grasp the reasoning behind such changes, diminishing the probability of disappointment.

All in all, effective client maintenance depends on a sensitive harmony between estimating procedures and a convincing offer. By fitting evaluating models to various client sections, offering motivating forces, and guaranteeing straightforwardness, organizations can make a strong groundwork. At the same time, areas of strength for a suggestion that integrates personalization, extraordinary help, persistent development, and instructive substance supports the explanations behind clients to remain faithful. In today's dynamic business landscape, a robust strategy for customer retention is formed by integrating these components, guided by data-driven insights and efficient communication.

Chapter 2 Implementing Effective

Customer Retention Strategies

Executing viable client maintenance techniques is vital for the drawn out progress of any business. Retaining existing customers goes beyond just acquiring new ones; it centers around building enduring associations with existing ones. This guarantees a consistent income stream as well as upgrades brand dedication and backing. In this article, we will investigate key procedures for effective client maintenance.

1. Grasp Your Clients:

Understanding your customers is the first step in keeping them. Use client information and examination to acquire bits of knowledge into their inclinations, conduct, and needs. By understanding your clients on a more profound level, you can tailor your items, administrations, and correspondence to all the more likely measures up to their assumptions.

2. Customized Correspondence:

Nonexclusive correspondence is a relic of past times. In the competitive market of today, personalization is essential. Use client names in messages, suggest items in view of their past buys, and send designated advancements. Customers feel valued when they receive personalized communication, which also strengthens their connection to your brand.

3. Outstanding Client support:

Giving extraordinary client care is one of the best maintenance procedures. Address client requests expeditiously, resolve issues proficiently, and go above and beyond to surpass assumptions. A positive client support experience can transform a disappointed client into a dependable promoter for your image.

4. Steadfastness Projects:

Carrying out a very much planned dependability program empowers rehash business. Offer prizes, limits, or select admittance to steadfast clients. These projects make a feeling of selectiveness and appreciation, encouraging a more grounded connection among clients and your image.

5. Ceaseless Commitment:

Remain top-of-mind by keeping up with consistent commitment with your clients. Routinely update them on new items, advancements, or industry news. Online entertainment, bulletins, and designated content are compelling apparatuses for continuous correspondence.

6. Collect feedback and act on it:

Urge clients to give input on their encounters. Use studies, audits, and virtual entertainment to accumulate bits of knowledge. Examine this feedback and make any necessary changes. Clients appreciate when their perspectives are esteemed, and tending to their interests constructs trust.

7. Fabricate a Local area:

Make a feeling of the local area around your image. Customers can connect with one another, share their experiences, and become advocates for your products by participating in online forums and social media platforms. A sense of belonging is cultivated through community development, which is crucial to customer retention.

8. Expect Client Needs:

Proactively expect and address client needs before they even express them. Utilize prescient examination to recognize examples and patterns in client conduct. This empowers you to offer important arrangements, improving the general client experience.

9. Predictable Marking:

Keep up with consistency in marking across all touchpoints. From your site to web-based entertainment and bundling, a strong brand picture fabricates trust. Your brand's identity is bolstered by consistency, and customers will remember and recognize your company.

10. Reward References:

Urge existing clients to allude others by carrying out reference programs. Offer motivators, like limits or selective access, for effective references. Verbal exchange showcasing stays quite possibly the most useful asset, and fulfilled clients are probably going to get new business.

11. Make smart use of technology:

Influence innovation to smooth out the client experience. To keep track of interactions, automate procedures, and personalize communication, implement CRM systems. Man-made consciousness can likewise be utilized for prescient examination and chatbots, improving effectiveness and responsiveness.

12. Offer Adaptable Installment Choices:

Offer customers a variety of payment options. Payment gateways, subscription models, and installment plans are all examples of this. Offering decisions takes care of various client inclinations and makes the buying system more advantageous.

13. Screen Client Beat:

Consistently screen and examine client beat rates. Distinguish the motivations behind why clients are leaving and make remedial moves. Understanding the agitate designs assists in creating designated systems with holding in danger clients.

14. Surprise and Satisfaction:

Incidentally shock your clients with surprising advantages or gifts. This could be a customized card to say thanks, a little rebate on their birthday, or select admittance to another item. These amazements make positive feelings and significant encounters.

15. Versatile Estimating Models:

Change evaluating models in view of client conduct and market patterns. Present layered evaluating, reliability limits, or membership plans. Adaptability in evaluating guarantees that clients see your contributions as significant and customized to their necessities.

effective client maintenance requires a diverse methodology. It entails getting to know your customers, giving them exceptional service, putting loyalty programs into place, and keeping them engaged with personalized communication. Businesses can cultivate a loyal customer base that lasts and expands over time by consistently providing value and fostering positive relationships. Keep in mind, the key isn't simply procuring clients yet keeping them fulfilled and putting resources into the drawn out venture with your image.

Personalization and Customization

Personalization and customization have become necessary parts of our advanced lives, affecting different ventures and forming our encounters in exceptional ways. These terms are frequently utilized conversely, yet they have unmistakable subtleties that influence how organizations take special care of individual inclinations and necessities.

At its center, personalization includes fitting encounters or content in light of expansive qualities like socioeconomics, area, and ways of behaving. For example, online retailers might utilize personalization to suggest items in light of a client's perusing history or buy conduct. This approach intends to upgrade client commitment and fulfillment by introducing applicable substance.

Then again, customization makes personalization a stride further, permitting people to effectively pick and change components as indicated by their inclinations. This can go from choosing the shade of an item to designing programming connection points. Users feel more in control of their own experiences when they can customize their experiences.

The retail scene has seen a significant change through the execution of customized and tweaked methodologies. In order to provide personalized product recommendations and a seamless shopping experience, e-commerce giants use sophisticated algorithms to analyze user data. This not just smoothes out the dynamic cycle for buyers yet additionally improves the general shopping experience, frequently prompting expanded client faithfulness.

The ascent of web-based features in media outlets represents the force of personalization. Stages like Netflix and Spotify influence client information to arrange customized content proposals, guaranteeing that clients are given shows, films, or music custom-made to their inclinations. This keeps clients connected as well as encourages a more profound association between the stage and its crowd.

In the domain of innovation, the customization of programming connection points has become progressively predominant. Users can now personalize their digital environments by customizing operating systems, applications, smartphones, and even more. This takes care of individual style as well as upgrades convenience by fitting points of interaction to client inclinations.

Training has likewise embraced personalization and customization to take special care of assorted learning styles and inclinations. Versatile learning stages use information investigation to comprehend individual learning designs, giving modified growth opportunities that adjust to every understudy's speed and cognizance level. This custom-made approach further develops learning results as well as advances a really captivating and understudy driven instructive climate.

Regardless of the horde benefits, the inescapable reception of personalization and customization raises worries about protection and information security. The assortment and investigation of tremendous measures of client information to drive personalization endeavors have ignited banters about the moral ramifications of such practices. Finding some kind of harmony between conveying custom-made encounters and defending client protection stays a basic test for organizations and policymakers the same.

Besides, there is a scarcely discernible difference between giving helpful suggestions and making channel bubbles that limit openness to different points of view. Over-dependence on personalization calculations may unintentionally trap people in close quarters, building up their current convictions and inclinations. This brings up issues about the cultural effect of personalization on data utilization and the likely ramifications for vote based talk.

As innovation keeps on propelling, the eventual fate of personalization and customization holds invigorating conceivable outcomes. Expanded reality (AR) and computer generated reality (VR) advances are ready to alter customized encounters, offering vivid and custom-made communications in different spaces, from retail to diversion. The combination of man-made brainpower and AI will additionally refine personalization calculations, empowering more precise expectations and suggestions.

All in all, personalization and customization have reshaped how we associate with items, administrations, and data. From customized shopping suggestions to adjustable advanced interfaces, these methodologies have improved client encounters across assorted enterprises. Be that as it may, as we explore this period of customized encounters, it is basic to address moral worries, guaranteeing a harmony among customization and security. The continuous development of innovation guarantees much more customized and vivid encounters, denoting a dynamic and extraordinary excursion for people and ventures the same.

Loyalty Programs and Proactive Customer Support

Steadfastness programs and proactive client service are indispensable parts of current organizations endeavoring to assemble enduring associations with their clients. In addition to increasing customer satisfaction, these strategies significantly increase brand loyalty and long-term profitability.

Dedication Projects:

Faithfulness programs have developed past customary punch cards and paper coupons. In the computerized age, organizations influence modern frameworks to compensate and hold clients. Points, discounts, or exclusive access to products or services are frequently included in these programs. The essential objective is to support rehash business and encourage a feeling of steadfastness among clients.

One vital benefit of reliability programs is the capacity to gather important client information. By following buying propensities and inclinations, organizations can customize their contributions, making a really captivating and custom-made insight. This customized approach reinforces the client business relationship as well as improves the probability of clients proceeding to pick a specific brand.

Besides, dependability programs act as a strong promoting instrument. By offering restrictive arrangements or early admittance to new items, organizations can make a feeling of selectiveness, causing clients to feel appreciated and esteemed. This positive feeling frequently converts into expanded client support, as fulfilled clients are bound to prescribe a brand to other people.

Nonetheless, the progress of devotion programs depends on their straightforwardness and straightforwardness. Customer dissatisfaction and disengagement can result from unclear terms or complicated structures. Finding some kind of harmony between alluring prizes and simplicity of interest is significant for expanding the effect of steadfastness programs.

Proactive Support for Customers:

Customer needs should be anticipated and addressed before they become apparent or problematic in order to provide proactive customer support.

Rather than trusting that clients will connect with issues, organizations step up to the plate and give help and direction. This approach is a proactive method for upgrading the general client experience.

Predictive analysis is an important part of providing proactive customer service. Businesses can identify potential issues before they become more serious by making use of data analytics. For instance, proactive measures can be taken to address the underlying issue or provide solutions to affected customers if a particular product has a history of customer complaints. This not only stops widespread dissatisfaction but also demonstrates a dedication to the well-being of customers.

One more feature of proactive help is instructive effort. Customers can be empowered to get the most out of their purchases by providing them with helpful advice, tutorials, and other relevant materials. This not just lessens the probability of disarray or disappointment yet in addition positions the business as a confided in guide, cultivating a feeling of dedication.

Online entertainment observing is likewise a significant component of proactive client care. By effectively checking on the web discussions, organizations can distinguish expected issues or concerns raised by clients. Answering quickly and openly to these worries shows straightforwardness and a guarantee to settling issues, which can emphatically influence the view of the brand.

Incorporation of Reliability Projects and Proactive Client care:

A powerful strategy that is focused on the customer can be developed by combining proactive customer support with loyalty programs. For example, a client who experiences an issue yet gets proactive help to determine it might feel an increased feeling of appreciation. Offering reliability program individuals selective admittance to sped up help benefits further supports the worth of cooperation.

In addition, the information gathered through reliability projects can illuminate proactive help endeavors. For instance, in the event that a dedicated client encounters an issue with a new buyer, the business can proactively contact and settle the issue expeditiously, forestalling any adverse consequence on the client's impression of the brand.

In the cutthroat scene of the present business world, the blend of reliability programs and proactive client care can be a unique advantage. Fabricating and keeping up with client steadfastness requires a comprehensive methodology that goes past value-based connections. By putting resources into methodologies that focus on consumer loyalty, organizations can hold their client base as well as transform fulfilled clients into energetic promoters. At last, the mix of dependability programs and proactive client care lines up with the more extensive objective of making a positive and noteworthy client experience.

Continuous Feedback and Improvement

Ceaseless criticism and improvement are urgent parts in upgrading client maintenance procedures. In the unique scene of business, where client assumptions develop quickly, it is fundamental to keep a proactive methodology. This article delves into strategies and benefits that businesses can utilize to strengthen their relationships with customers and examines the significance of continuous feedback and improvement in the context of customer retention.

Grasping Nonstop Criticism:

Nonstop input includes the predictable social occasion of data from clients all through their excursion with an item or administration. Not at all like conventional input strategies that depend on occasional studies, nonstop criticism is a continuous cycle that empowers constant bits of knowledge into client encounters. This iterative methodology permits organizations to adjust quickly to changing client needs and inclinations.

The Job of Consistent Improvement:

Constant improvement supplements criticism by making an interpretation of assembled experiences into noteworthy procedures. It includes a repeating cycle of breaking down input, distinguishing regions for upgrade, executing changes, and afterward reconsidering the effect. This iterative circle cultivates a culture of versatility and development, critical for remaining ahead in the serious market.

Procedures for Ceaseless Input and Improvement:

Ongoing Input Instruments:

Carrying out continuous criticism systems, for example, chatbots or moment reviews, engages organizations to catch client feelings right now of association. This quickness empowers brief reactions and changes, building up a client driven approach.

Information Examination and Client Bits of knowledge:

Utilizing progressed investigation instruments permits organizations to gather important bits of knowledge from client information. Patterns, preferences, and behaviors can be analyzed to pinpoint areas in need of improvement. This information driven approach guarantees key dynamics in view of substantial proof.

Mapping the Customer's Journey:

Understanding the client venture is instrumental in upgrading touchpoints. By delineating each cooperation from attention to post-buy, organizations gain a comprehensive perspective on the client experience. This understanding guides in pinpointing trouble spots and open doors for refinement.

Training and feedback from employees:

Inward criticism is essentially as crucial as outside input. Representatives, being the bleeding edge envoys, can give important bits of knowledge into client communications. Normal preparation programs in light of criticism guarantee that the group is prepared to meet developing client assumptions.

Iterative Item Advancement:

Constant improvement stretches out to the items or administrations advertised. Iterative improvement in light of client criticism guarantees that contributions stay significant and lined up with market requests. This proactive methodology forestalls out of date quality and exhibits a guarantee to consumer loyalty.

Advantages of Nonstop Criticism and Improvement in Client Maintenance:
Expanded Consumer loyalty:

Resolving issues instantly and making enhancements in view of criticism straightforwardly add to higher consumer loyalty. Fulfilled clients are bound to stay faithful and supporters for the brand.

Proactive Issue Goal:

Distinguishing and settling issues progressively keeps client dissatisfaction from rising. This proactive methodology limits the gamble of losing clients because of annoying issues.

Upgraded Client Unwaveringly:

Persistent improvement makes a positive input circle, encouraging client steadfastness. At the point when clients witness a brand's obligation to refining its contributions in view of their criticism, they feel esteemed and are bound to remain steadfast.

Upper hand:

Businesses that can quickly adapt gain a competitive advantage in a market that is constantly shifting. Persistent criticism and improvement guarantee that an organization stays spry and responsive, situating itself as a forerunner in consumer loyalty.

Streamlined Client Experience:

By refining touchpoints and adjusting contributions to client assumptions, organizations can convey a streamlined client experience. A consistent and charming experience is a critical consideration holding clients over the long haul.

Difficulties and Contemplations:

Despite the significant advantages, implementing strategies for continuous improvement and feedback comes with difficulties. Businesses must balance the need for feedback with the fatigue of customer surveys, guarantee data privacy, and effectively manage the influx of feedback data. Furthermore, deciphering input precisely and keeping away from automatic responses are pivotal to keeping a key and estimated approach.

In the domain of client maintenance, persistent criticism and improvement go about as the bedrock of practical achievement. The cooperative connection between get-together ongoing experiences and carrying out essential upgrades makes a client driven biological system. Organizations that embrace this iterative cycle hold their client base as well as position themselves as versatile, client centered elements in the serious market. As client assumptions keep on advancing, the obligation to consistent criticism and improvement stays an irreplaceable apparatus for organizations endeavoring to hold as well as to flourish in their client connections.

Chapter 3
Utilizing Technology for Customer Retention

Using innovation for client maintenance is a basic part of current business procedure. In the present dynamic and serious market, where gaining new clients can be exorbitant, holding existing ones becomes basic for supported achievement. Utilizing innovation can altogether upgrade client maintenance endeavors, giving organizations apparatuses to fabricate enduring connections, further develop consumer loyalty, and eventually help reliability.

Through data analytics, technology plays a significant role in customer retention. By tackling the force of huge information, organizations can acquire important bits of knowledge into client conduct, inclinations, and patterns. Investigating this information permits organizations to make customized encounters, tailor their items or administrations to individual requirements, and expect client assumptions. For example, proposal calculations can recommend significant items in view of a client's previous buys, improving their general shopping experience and cultivating dependability.

Client relationship the executives (CRM) frameworks assume a critical part in using innovation for client maintenance. These stages empower organizations to concentrate client data, track connections, and oversee connections productively. By having a complete perspective on every client, organizations can convey customized correspondence, address explicit necessities, and resolve issues expeditiously. Also, CRM frameworks work with designated showcasing efforts, guaranteeing that advancements and messages reverberate with the right crowd, prompting expanded client commitment and faithfulness.

Mechanization is another innovative device that essentially influences client maintenance. Mechanizing routine cycles, like request affirmations, delivering warnings, and client support requests, saves time as well as guarantees steady and opportune correspondence. Chatbots, fueled by computerized reasoning, can deal with fundamental client inquiries, giving moment reactions and opening up HR to zero in on additional complicated issues. This smoothed out and productive correspondence improves consumer loyalty and adds to a positive generally speaking experience.

Virtual entertainment stages are instrumental in keeping areas of strength for clients. Social media can be used by businesses to build a community around their brand as well as for marketing. Drawing in with clients through friendly channels permits organizations to get constant criticism, address concerns immediately, and exhibit their obligation to consumer loyalty. Moreover, virtual entertainment gives a stage to clients to share their encounters, making client produced content that can additionally advance brand unwaveringly.

Portable applications have become vital to client maintenance techniques. With the pervasiveness of cell phones, organizations can make customized and advantageous encounters for their clients through devoted versatile applications. These applications can offer faithfulness programs, restrictive limits, and customized content, furnishing clients with added motivating forces to remain faithful to the brand. Pop-up messages through portable applications likewise empower organizations to remain top-of-mind, helping clients to remember new items, advancements, or impending occasions. Viable correspondence is central in client maintenance, and innovation works with consistent correspondence channels. For instance, email marketing continues to be an effective method for fostering relationships with customers. To encourage customer engagement and loyalty, automated email campaigns can be designed to send targeted messages based on customer behavior, preferences, or milestones. Incorporating email crusades with client information from CRM frameworks guarantees that correspondences are pertinent and opportune.

Increased reality (AR) and computer generated reality (VR) advancements offer imaginative ways of connecting with clients and improve their experience. For instance, AR can be utilized to permit clients to envision items in their own current circumstance prior to pursuing a buy choice. VR can make vivid encounters, like virtual item shows or virtual voyages through actual areas, having an enduring impact on clients. These innovations separate a brand as well as add to a noteworthy and positive client experience.

Online business stages benefit altogether from innovation driven client maintenance systems. Personalization motors on these stages investigate client conduct, buy history, and inclinations to prescribe items customized to individual clients. In addition, features like one-click ordering, saved preferences, and simple returns make shopping a breeze and make customers more likely to come back for more.

Consistently looking for client input through overviews and surveys is fundamental for understanding their fulfillment levels and distinguishing regions for development. Innovation improves on the criticism interaction by empowering organizations to make online overviews, screen web-based entertainment audits, and dissect feelings through opinion investigation instruments. This important input circle permits organizations to resolve issues proactively, feature their obligation to consumer loyalty, and show that client suppositions are esteemed.

Using technology to keep customers is a multifaceted strategy that includes data analytics, customer relationship management (CRM) systems, automation, social media engagement, mobile applications, efficient communication channels, augmented and virtual reality, and personalized e-commerce. By decisively integrating these innovations, organizations can establish a client driven climate, upgrade consumer loyalty, and encourage long haul steadfastness. In the present computerized age, remaining ahead in the serious scene requires securing new clients as well as utilizing mechanical progressions to hold and sustain existing ones.

Customer Relationship Management (CRM) Systems

As a strategic tool for managing interactions and relationships with customers, customer relationship management (CRM) systems are essential to modern business. These frameworks have advanced altogether throughout the long term, changing from straightforward information bases to refined stages that coordinate different parts of client commitment. We'll take a comprehensive look at CRM systems' key components, advantages, drawbacks, and potential future trends.

Parts of CRM Frameworks:
Client Information The board:

Fundamental to CRM frameworks is the powerful administration of client information. Information about customer interactions, preferences, and purchase histories, among other things, can be stored and organized in these platforms' repositories. The basis for personalized and targeted marketing campaigns is this data.

Lead The board:

CRM systems aid in the management and tracking of leads all the way through the sales funnel. This includes catching leads, relegating them to agents, and checking their movement through different stages until change. Mechanization highlights smooth out these cycles, improving effectiveness and decreasing manual responsibility.

Deals Mechanization:

Robotization is a vital element of CRM frameworks, especially in deals processes. From lead sustaining to statement age and request handling, mechanization speeds up work processes, permitting outreach groups to zero in on high-esteem errands. In addition to increasing productivity, this also lowers the likelihood of human error.

Automation in Marketing:

By automating processes like email marketing, social media posting, and customer segmentation, CRM systems enable targeted marketing campaigns. This empowers organizations to convey customized content to explicit client sections, expanding the adequacy of showcasing endeavors.

Support and Service for Customers:

Giving uncommon client support is fundamentally important for organizations, and CRM frameworks assume an essential part in accomplishing this. They smooth out client care processes, empower proficient ticket the board, and engage support groups with an exhaustive perspective on client communications. This outcomes in quicker issue goals and improved consumer loyalty.

Advantages of CRM Frameworks:

Improved Relationships with Customers:

CRM frameworks enable organizations to fabricate more grounded, more customized associations with their clients. Companies can improve customer loyalty and satisfaction by tailoring their communication and offerings by comprehending customer preferences and behavior.

Upgraded Client Experience:

A consistent and customized client experience is a sign of effective CRM execution. CRM systems ensure consistency and quality from the first interaction to post-purchase support, fostering a positive customer experience overall.

Expanded Effectiveness and Efficiency:

Operational efficiency is significantly enhanced by automation in CRM systems. Deals, showcasing, and client care groups can robotize tedious undertakings, permitting them to zero in on essential exercises that require human mediation. This resulted in expanded efficiency across the association.

Information Driven Navigation:

CRM frameworks give important bits of knowledge through investigation and revealing apparatuses. Organizations can examine client patterns, track deals execution, and assess the adequacy of advertising efforts. Informed by information, leaders can devise procedures that line up with client assumptions and market elements.

Versatility and Adaptability:

Present day CRM frameworks are intended to scale with the development of a business. Whether extending client bases, adding new items, or entering new business sectors, these frameworks can adjust to changing business necessities, giving the adaptability required in powerful conditions.

Problems Related to CRM Systems:

Joining Intricacy:

Coordinating CRM frameworks with existing innovations can be complex and challenging. Consistent incorporation is urgent for amplifying the advantages of CRM, however it frequently requires cautious preparation and specialized ability.

Information Security and Protection Concerns:

With the rising accentuation on information protection, organizations should focus on the security of client data inside CRM frameworks. Consistence with guidelines, for example, GDPR is vital for building and keeping up with entrust with clients.

Client Reception:

The outcome of CRM frameworks relies upon client reception. Protection from change and an absence of understanding about the framework's capacities can prevent its viability. Complete preparation programs and progressing support are pivotal for beating this test.

Cost of Execution and Support:

Executing a powerful CRM framework includes huge forthright expenses, including programming, preparing, and customization. The total cost of ownership is further inflated by regular updates and maintenance. Little and medium sized undertakings might find these costs testing.

Customization Intricacy:

While customization is a critical strength of CRM frameworks, it can likewise present difficulties. Adjusting the requirement for customized arrangements no sweat of purpose requires cautious thought to guarantee ideal framework execution.

Future Patterns in CRM:

Integration of AI and machine learning:

The mix of man-made reasoning and AI is set to alter CRM. Predictive analytics will be improved, routine tasks will be automated, and more precise insights into customer behavior will be provided by these technologies.

High level Client Division:

Advanced algorithms will be used in future CRM systems to create more granular customer segments. Businesses can deliver highly targeted and personalized experiences to individual customers or micro-segments with this level of segmentation.

Omni-Channel Commitment:

The emphasis on omni-channel client commitment will increase, with CRM frameworks turning out to be considerably more proficient at overseeing associations across different channels consistently. This guarantees a steady and incorporated insight for clients, no matter what the correspondence channel.

More prominent Accentuation on Client Maintenance:

While securing new clients is fundamental, future CRM procedures will put a more noteworthy accentuation on client maintenance. Proactive measures, for example, customized devotion programs and designated re-commitment crusades, will be coordinated into CRM frameworks.

Blockchain for Information Security:

Blockchain innovation is supposed to assume a part in upgrading information security inside CRM frameworks. Concerns about data breaches and unauthorized access can be addressed by its decentralized and immutable nature, which can provide an additional layer of protection for customer information. customer-centric strategies are based on CRM systems, which are essential to modern business operations. As innovation keeps on advancing, these frameworks will assume an undeniably modern part in overseeing and improving client connections. Be that as it may, organizations should explore difficulties and remain receptive to arising patterns to completely use the capability of CRM in a steadily changing business scene.

Data Analytics for Customer Insights

Information investigation for client experiences is a useful asset that organizations influence to acquire a more profound comprehension of their clients. In the advanced business scene, where information is bountiful and various, bridging this data can give significant experiences that drive vital navigation, improve consumer loyalty, and lift in general business execution.

Getting a handle on customer data:

At the center of information investigation for client experiences is the immense measure of information produced by client associations. Purchase history, website interactions, social media engagement, and other data may be included. By accumulating and examining this data, organizations can uncover examples, patterns, and connections that uncover significant bits of knowledge into client conduct.

Personalization and segmentation:

One critical part of information examination for client bits of knowledge is division. Organizations can partition their client base into unmistakable sections in light of different measures like socioeconomics, area, buy history, or inclinations. This division takes into account more designated and customized showcasing procedures.

For instance, a retailer can dissect buy history to recognize sections of clients who habitually purchase comparative items. By understanding the inclinations of these portions, the retailer can fit advertising efforts to more readily reverberate with each gathering, improving the probability of commitment and transformation.

Prescient Examination:

Prescient investigation is one more urgent component of utilizing client information. By utilizing verifiable information and progressed investigation methods, organizations can make forecasts about future client conduct. Forecasting future purchases, recognizing potential customer churn, and comprehending the factors that influence customer satisfaction are all examples of this.

For example, an online business stage could utilize prescient examination to guess which items a client is probably going to be keen on in light of their past way of behaving. This empowers the stage to suggest significant items, making a more customized and pleasant shopping experience.

Client Excursion Planning:

Information examination permits organizations to delineate the client venture thoroughly. Understanding the different touchpoints and communications a client has with a brand gives significant bits of knowledge into their experience. Organizations can distinguish trouble spots, areas of progress, and snapshots of enjoyment all through the client venture.

By examining client venture information, organizations can advance their cycles, smooth out connections, and eventually upgrade generally consumer loyalty. An online service provider might, for instance, look at user interactions to find problems with the onboarding process. This would make the experience for new customers easier and more effective.

Criticism Investigation:

Client input, whether from studies, surveys, or web-based entertainment, is a goldmine of data. Information examination instruments can break down this criticism at scale, extricating opinion, recognizing normal topics, and pinpointing regions for development.

For example, a neighborliness business can utilize feeling examination on client surveys to comprehend how visitors see their administrations. On the off chance that there's a predictable notice of a particular issue, for example, slow help in the café, the business can make designated moves to address and correct the issue.

Ongoing Investigation:

The importance of real-time analytics is growing in the fast-paced business environment. The capacity to break down client information continuously permits organizations to answer immediately to changing patterns and client needs.

For instance, a retail site might utilize ongoing examination to screen site traffic and distinguish unexpected spikes in interest for a specific item. This data can set off quick changes in showcasing systems, stock administration, and site content to profit by the pattern.

Information Security and Protection:

While information examination gives huge advantages, it additionally raises worries about information security and protection. Organizations should explore the sensitive equilibrium of using client information to upgrade encounters while guaranteeing hearty safety efforts and consistence with security guidelines.

Carrying out encryption, access controls, and anonymizing delicate data are vital stages in protecting client information. Additionally, straightforward correspondence about information use and giving clients command over their information can cultivate trust and moderate protection concerns.

Considerations and Challenges:

In spite of the groundbreaking capability of information examination for client experiences, organizations face difficulties as far as information quality, mix of different information sources, and the requirement for talented information experts. It's fundamental for associations to put resources into information administration rehearses, information quality confirmation, and continuous preparation for their groups to separate significant bits of knowledge from the information storm successfully.

In the business world, data analytics for customer insights is a game-changer. By tackling the force of information, organizations can figure out their clients on a more profound level, customize encounters, and go with informed choices. As innovation keeps on propelling, the job of information examination in forming client driven methodologies will just turn out to be more noticeable, offering organizations an upper hand in a dynamic and developing business sector.

Automation in Retention Processes

Streamlining processes, improving customer retention strategies, and ensuring a seamless customer experience are all made possible by automation. In the domain of client maintenance, where building enduring connections is foremost, robotization ends up being a unique advantage. This article dives into the heap ways robotization is changing maintenance processes, offering proficiency, personalization, and supported client steadfastness.

1. Information driven Bits of knowledge:

The foundation for effective data analytics in retention processes is automation. Businesses can gain profound insights into customer behaviors, preferences, and interactions by automating data collection and analysis. This information driven approach empowers organizations to expect client needs, distinguish examples, and designer maintenance methodologies likewise. For example, a mechanized framework can follow by history, commitment measurements, and input, giving an exhaustive perspective on every client's excursion.

2. Customized Correspondence:

Compelling correspondence is the foundation of client maintenance, and mechanization works with customized communications at scale. Mechanized showcasing stages use client information to send designated messages, offers, and proposals. Whether it's a customized email, a custom-made markdown, or a convenient item idea, computerization guarantees that clients get content pertinent to their inclinations, cultivating a feeling of association and worth.

3. Dynamic Client Division:

Computerization considers dynamic and ongoing client division. Customers can be divided into groups by a variety of factors, such as their purchasing habits, demographics, or level of engagement. This division empowers organizations to come up with explicit maintenance methodologies for various client gatherings. For instance, high-esteem clients could get selective advantages, while in danger clients could be focused on with customized re-commitment crusades.

4. Robotized Unwaveringly Projects:

Automating loyalty programs takes them to a new level of effectiveness for retaining customers. Robotized frameworks can follow and oversee faithfulness focuses, issue compensations, and send notices to clients about their dedication status. This improves on the organization of unwaveringly programs as well as guarantees a consistent and charming experience for clients, upgrading their obligation to the brand.

5. Chatbots for Moment Backing:

Robotization in client maintenance stretches out to offering moments and effective help. Artificial intelligence-powered chatbots can answer questions, resolve problems, and provide information round-the-clock.

This not only enhances the overall customer experience but also increases customer satisfaction. Computerized chatbots can deal with routine inquiries, passing on human specialists to zero in on additional mind boggling and customized corporations.

6. Prescient Investigation for Stir Anticipation:

One of the basic difficulties in client maintenance is foreseeing and forestalling agitation. Mechanization, combined with prescient investigation, empowers organizations to recognize potential beat pointers. Automated systems can identify customers who are likely to leave by analyzing previous data and customer behavior. This enables businesses to intervene with targeted retention efforts before it is too late.

7. Automated Comments from Customers:

Understanding consumer loyalty and social occasion input is vital to maintenance. Computerization smoothes out the criticism interaction via consequently sending studies, gathering reactions, and breaking down the information. Continuous input empowers organizations to resolve issues immediately and make information driven enhancements. This iterative input circle adds to constant improvement of items and administrations, eventually supporting client dependability.

8. Work process Computerization for Effectiveness:

In the background, work process computerization improves inner cycles, adding to by and large effectiveness in client maintenance endeavors. Whether it's computerizing request handling, overseeing client data sets, or planning cross-departmental endeavors, work process mechanization guarantees that organizations work consistently. This proficiency converts into speedier reaction times, customized administrations, and a more lithe way to deal with client maintenance.

9. Re-commitment Missions:

Robotized re-commitment crusades are instrumental in reconnecting with torpid or in danger clients. By setting up triggers in view of client conduct, organizations can naturally start designated missions to win back clients. This could incorporate customized offers, updates, or selective admittance to new highlights. Computerization guarantees that these re-commitment endeavors are convenient and customized to every client's special circumstance.

10. System Integration with CRM:

A centralized repository for customer data is made possible by automation's seamless integration with CRM systems. This reconciliation empowers a comprehensive perspective on client communications across different touchpoints. Whether it's a deals call, support ticket, or online entertainment communication, robotization guarantees that each client cooperation is recorded and dissected, adding to a more educated and customized maintenance technique.

Robotization in maintenance processes is a groundbreaking power in current client relationships with the board. From information driven experiences to customized correspondence, dynamic division, and work process advancement, computerization enables organizations to construct more grounded, enduring associations with their clients. As innovation keeps on propelling, the collaboration among robotization and client maintenance procedures will without a doubt develop, giving organizations progressively refined instruments to sustain and hold their client base.

Chapter 4
Case Studies and Success Stories

Client maintenance is a basic part of any business procedure, as it straightforwardly influences long haul achievement and benefit. In order to keep current customers happy, loyal, and choosing their products or services, businesses spend a lot of money on various customer retention strategies. Contextual analyses and examples of overcoming adversity assume a crucial part in understanding and exhibiting powerful systems that have yielded positive outcomes in holding clients.

1. Grasping Client Maintenance:
Understanding customer retention is essential before diving into case studies. It goes past just obtaining clients; it

includes building enduring connections, surpassing assumptions, and ceaselessly conveying esteem. A definitive objective is to lessen client stir, keeping them drawn in and faithful after some time.

2. Contextual analysis 1: Amazon Prime's Faithfulness Program:

Amazon Prime stands apart as a perfect representation of fruitful client maintenance through a steadfastness program. Amazon has created a compelling value proposition for its customers by providing benefits like free shipping, exclusive deals, and streaming services. This contextual investigation features how putting resources into a reliability program can essentially improve consumer loyalty and dependability.

3. Example of overcoming adversity 1: Starbucks Prizes Program:

Starbucks' portable application and prizes program have been instrumental in making clients want more. The application works on the requesting system as well as offers customized advancements in light of the client's inclinations. This example of overcoming adversity underscores the significance of utilizing innovation to upgrade the client experience and construct reliability.

4. 2nd Case Study: The Outstanding Customer Service of Zappos:

Zappos, an internet based shoe and dress retailer, is famous for its outstanding client support. The organization's contextual analysis exhibits how blowing away in client care can be areas of strength for cultivating devotion. The customer service representatives at Zappos have the authority to go above and beyond what customers expect, making their experience memorable and positive, which helps them stay with the company.

5. Example of overcoming adversity 2: Spotify's Customized Proposals:

Spotify's progress in client maintenance is intently attached to its customized suggestion calculations. By investigating client conduct and inclinations, Spotify tailors music proposals, keeping clients drew in for longer periods. This example of overcoming adversity underscores the meaning of personalization in holding clients in the cutthroat streaming industry.

6. Contextual analysis 3: HubSpot's Inbound Advertising:

HubSpot's contextual analysis grandstands the viability of inbound advertising in client maintenance. By making significant substance, supporting leads, and giving instructive assets, HubSpot has constructed a local area around its image. This methodology draws in new clients as well as continues existing ones drawn in, encouraging a feeling of reliability.

7. Example of overcoming adversity 3: Apple's Biological system Reconciliation:

Apple's consistent mix of equipment and programming across its item setup is a demonstration of effective client maintenance. When a client puts resources into the Macintosh biological system, with gadgets like iPhones, Macintoshes, and iPads, the consistent experience and cross-gadget similarity boost them to stay inside the Mac environment. This example of overcoming adversity features the force of making an interconnected item biological system to hold clients.

8. 4th Case Study: Netflix's Information driven Content Suggestions:

The Netflix case study shows how data-driven content recommendations help keep customers coming back. By dissecting seeing propensities and inclinations, Netflix proposes content custom fitted to individual preferences. This customized approach keeps clients drawn in, diminishing the probability of stir. The contextual analysis accentuates the significance of utilizing information to upgrade client experience and fulfillment.

9. Example of overcoming adversity 4: Airbnb's People group Building:

Airbnb's outcome in client maintenance is established in its attention on local area building. The stage urges hosts and visitors to draw in with one another, encouraging a feeling of having a place. This example of overcoming adversity highlights the job of the local area and association in holding clients, particularly in the sharing economy.

contextual analyses and examples of overcoming adversity in client maintenance methods give important experiences into systems that have demonstrated viable in different ventures. From unwavering projects to extraordinary client assistance and customized encounters, these models exhibit that holding clients goes past value-based communications. Organizations that put resources into understanding and satisfying client needs are bound to fabricate enduring connections, guaranteeing supported outcome in the serious market scene. By gaining from these contextual investigations and examples of overcoming adversity, organizations can refine their client maintenance techniques and make a positive effect on their primary concern.

Examples of Successful Customer Retention

Client maintenance is a basic part of business achievement, and various organizations have carried out effective systems to keep their current clients connected with and fulfilled. How about we dive into a few prominent instances of powerful client maintenance across different businesses.

Amazon Prime:
Amazon Prime is a well-known case in point. By offering a membership administration that incorporates benefits like free delivery, selective arrangements, and admittance to real time features, Amazon has made a devout environment that urges clients to stay close by. Customers are more likely to stick with Amazon over other options due to the convenience and value-added services it provides.

Program for Starbucks Rewards:
Through its rewards program, Starbucks has perfected the art of keeping customers coming back. By offering focuses for each buy, customized offers, and a consistent versatile application

experience, Starbucks makes clients want more. The mental part of procuring rewards makes a feeling of achievement, making clients more learned to pick Starbucks over other bistros.

Apple's Biological system:

Apple has constructed a dependable client base by making an interconnected biological system of items and administrations. When a client puts resources into an iPhone, for instance, they are bound to stay with Macintosh for different gadgets and administrations, for example, MacBooks, iPads, Mac Watch, iCloud, and the Application Store. This consistent combination empowers long haul client connections.

Personalization on Netflix:

Netflix utilizes a modern proposal calculation that examines client conduct and inclinations. By proposing customized content ideas, Netflix upgrades the client experience, keeping clients drew in and fulfilled. This degree of personalization holds existing endorsers as well as draws in new ones, as clients consider the stage to be a wellspring of custom-made diversion.

Zappos Remarkable Client support:

Customer service at Zappos, an online shoe and clothing retailer, is renowned. They blow away in guaranteeing consumer loyalty, offering free delivery the two different ways and a 365-day merchandise exchange. Customers are more likely to return for future purchases as a result of this dedication to providing excellent service.

The Host Guarantee of Airbnb:

Airbnb has constructed an entrust with its host local area by carrying out the Host Assurance, which gives security up to $1 million in punitive fees. Hosts are encouraged to continue using the platform by this assurance, which ensures that their property is protected. This trust-building methodology adds to the general positive experience for the two hosts and visitors, prompting client maintenance.

Unwaveringly Projects in Aircrafts:

Aircrafts like Delta and Southwest have effectively carried out unwaveringly programs that award regular customers with miles, status levels, and elite advantages. Due to the perceived value of the rewards, these programs give customers a strong incentive to stay with a particular airline, even if it means paying slightly more.

Coca-Cola's Image Steadfastness:

Coca-Cola has kept areas of strength for a base for quite a long time through successful marking. The close to home association individuals have with the brand, joined with predictable quality and informing, keeps clients steadfast. Coca-Cola's promoting procedures center around making an encounter around their item, making it something other than a drink, however a piece of individuals' ways of life.

HubSpot's Inbound Promoting:

HubSpot, a showcasing mechanization and deals programming organization, tries doing what it proposes for others to do. Their inbound promoting philosophy draws in clients through significant substance, customized encounters, and client driven methodologies. HubSpot builds trust and customer loyalty by providing resources that assist businesses in succeeding, which results in long-term customer relationships.

Spotify's Client Driven Elements:

Spotify's user-centered features and constant innovation keep its users engaged. Highlights like customized playlists, Find Week after week, and cooperative playlists improve the general client experience. By remaining ahead in the cutthroat music streaming industry and understanding client inclinations, Spotify guarantees that clients stay faithful to the stage.

fruitful client maintenance procedures differ across enterprises, however they all offer normal components of offering some incentive, building trust, and making positive encounters. Whether through unwavering programs, excellent client support, or creative elements, these models exhibit the significance of putting resources into client connections for long haul business achievement.

Lessons Learned from Notable Case Studies

Client maintenance is a basic part of business achievement, and various contextual investigations have given important bits of knowledge into viable procedures. Looking at these cases offers important examples for organizations endeavoring to fabricate enduring associations with their clients.

One prominent contextual analysis is the progress of Amazon Prime. Amazon's membership administration furnishes clients with facilitated delivery as well as offers a scope of extra advantages, including web-based features and elite arrangements. The illustration here is that making an exhaustive dependability program can fundamentally upgrade client maintenance. By offering a heap of administrations that take special care of different requirements, organizations can make a convincing incentive that urges clients to remain locked in.

Likewise, Starbucks has succeeded in client maintenance through its prizes program. By offering free beverages, customized offers, and a consistent portable application experience, Starbucks has made a feeling of selectiveness and appreciation among its clients. The significance of personalization and convenience in retaining customers is exemplified in this case. Fitting prizes to individual inclinations and making the client experience frictionless can cultivate dependability.

On the other hand, the defeat of Blockbuster fills in as a useful example. The once-prevailing video rental chain neglected to adjust to changing buyer conduct and the ascent of internet web based. The example here is clear: organizations should develop with the times and embrace mechanical progressions to remain applicable. Neglecting to do so can prompt a decrease in client maintenance and eventually bring about business disappointment.

Another enlightening contextual investigation comes from Zappos, an internet based shoe and dress retailer.

Zappos focuses on outstanding client assistance, exceeding everyone's expectations to address client issues. The organization's obligation to a 365-day merchandise exchange and day in and day out client service has gained notoriety for unwavering quality and client centricity. The lesson learned from Zappos is that investing in exceptional customer service can result in positive word-of-mouth and long-term customer loyalty.

A later contextual investigation includes the outcome of membership based organizations like Netflix and Spotify. These stages have excelled at client maintenance by consistently giving new and select substance. The illustration here is that continuous commitment through ordinary updates and selective contributions can fundamentally affect client maintenance. Organizations ought to zero in on offering nonstop benefit to keep clients put resources into their administrations.

Contrastingly, the disappointment of Kodak in the computerized time features the significance of remaining in front of industry patterns. Kodak, a once-prevailing player in the photography market, neglected to adjust to the shift from film to computerized photography. This case accentuates the requirement for organizations to expect changes in shopper conduct and mechanical headways to keep up with client importance and maintenance.

Airbnb's excursion from a startup to a worldwide neighborliness goliath offers experiences into the force of local area building. By cultivating a feeling of having a place and trust among hosts and visitors, Airbnb has made a dedicated local area that reaches out to past exchanges. The illustration here is that building areas of strength for and around your image can upgrade client maintenance by making a feeling of reliability and shared values.

Besides, the progress of Apple in building areas of strength for any of the items and administrations exhibits the viability of strategically pitching and upselling. Apple clients frequently put resources into various Apple gadgets, making a consistent and interconnected client experience. By encouraging customers to remain within the brand ecosystem, this case study demonstrates the significance of offering complementary products or services to increase customer retention.

The disappointment of the New Coke send off during the 1980s fills in as an update that understanding client inclinations is central. Coca-Cola's choice to change its exemplary recipe without sufficiently measuring client opinion prompted a huge backfire. The illustration here is that organizations ought to direct careful statistical surveying and pay attention to client criticism prior to rolling out significant improvements to items or administrations that could affect maintenance.

examples gained from eminent contextual analyses in client maintenance methods highlight the meaning of versatility, personalization, client support, local area fabricating, and remaining receptive to advertise patterns. Organizations that focus on these angles are better situated to fabricate enduring associations with their clients, cultivating devotion and guaranteeing long haul achievement.

Chapter 5 Challenges in Customer Retention

Client maintenance is a basic part of any business, introducing the two valuable open doors and difficulties. While getting new clients is fundamental, holding existing ones is similarly significant for supported achievement. Nonetheless, accomplishing client maintenance isn't without its obstacles. This article investigates a portion of the critical difficulties organizations face in holding their client base.

1. Intense rivalry in the market:
In the present globalized economy, organizations face furious rivalry, making it trying to hold clients. With various choices accessible, clients can undoubtedly change to a contender offering more ideal arrangements or prevalent administrations. This comes down on organizations to persistently develop and improve their contributions to remain ahead on the lookout.

2. Developing Client Assumptions:
Technology advancements and shifts in social trends are the driving forces

behind the constant shift in customer expectations. Clients presently anticipate customized encounters, consistent collaborations across different channels, and moment answers for their concerns. Businesses must quickly adapt in order to meet these changing expectations; failing to do so can result in customer dissatisfaction and attrition.

3. Overload of communication:

In the period of data, clients are besieged with messages from different sources. It can be difficult to effectively communicate with customers through this noise. Organizations should track down the right harmony between keeping in contact with clients and staying away from correspondence over-burden, which can prompt bothering and separation.

4. Absence of Client Commitment:

Client commitment is urgent for maintenance, yet numerous organizations battle to keep their clients effectively involved. Absence of commitment can result from inadequate correspondence, tedious substance, or an inability to grasp the client's necessities. Building significant associations with clients requires an essential methodology that goes past value-based corporations.

5. Value Responsiveness:

Pricing is an important part of keeping customers coming back, but it can also be hard. Customers are frequently price-sensitive, and they can be turned off by any perception of unfair pricing or poor value. Businesses must navigate the delicate task of striking a balance between competitive pricing and maintaining profitability.

6. Nature of Client care:

Client care assumes a significant part in client maintenance. Unfortunate help, whether it be slow reaction times, lacking issue goals, or antagonistic corporations, can prompt client disappointment. Recognizing that a single negative experience can have a lasting impact on customer loyalty, businesses must invest in training and technology to ensure high-quality customer service.

7. Moving Purchaser Loyalties:

Buyer devotion is turning out to be more subtle in a time where decisions flourish. Clients are progressively ready to switch brands in the event that they view as a superior other option. Constructing and keeping up with unwaveringly expects organizations to reliably convey esteem, surpass assumptions, and encourage profound associations with their clients.

8. Information Security Concerns:

During a time where individual information is profoundly esteemed, worries about information security can influence client trust. Customer churn and eroded trust can result from a single data breach or improper handling of customer information. Organizations should put resources into hearty online protection measures and straightforward correspondence to address these worries and defend client trust.

9. Restricted Client Input:

Understanding client needs and inclinations is fundamental for maintenance, however organizations frequently face difficulties in acquiring significant client criticism. It's possible that the limited responses to surveys or reviews won't give you a complete picture of how customers feel. Utilizing assorted criticism channels and effectively looking for client information can assist with tending to this test.

10. Financial Vulnerability:

Outer variables, like financial slumps or worldwide emergencies, can fundamentally affect client maintenance. During intense financial times, clients might scale back costs, prompting diminished unwaveringly. Organizations should be deft in adjusting their techniques to explore monetary vulnerabilities and hold client dedication even in testing times.

All in all, client maintenance is a complex test that requires a comprehensive methodology from organizations. Adjusting to advertise elements, understanding advancing client assumptions, and resolving explicit issues, for example, correspondence over-burden and information security concerns are pivotal. By focusing on client commitment, conveying quality help, and remaining receptive to showcase patterns, organizations can defeat these difficulties and assemble enduring associations with their clients.

Identifying and Addressing Common Challenges

Recognizing and tending to normal difficulties in client maintenance strategies is urgent for organizations meaning to encourage long haul client connections and expand productivity. While client maintenance is fundamental for supported achievement, different obstructions can prevent these endeavors. Let's look at some common obstacles and effective ways to get around them.

One of the essential difficulties in client maintenance is figuring out client assumptions. As business sectors advance and shopper inclinations shift, remaining sensitive to changing assumptions turns out to be progressively intricate. Consistently gathering and dissecting client criticism through overviews, surveys, and direct correspondence channels can give important experiences. This data permits organizations to adjust their maintenance methodologies to line up with client assumptions and inclinations.

The lack of personalization in customer interactions is another common issue. Clients today expect fitted encounters that take special care of their singular necessities and inclinations. Advanced customer relationship management (CRM) systems can help businesses effectively collect and use customer data. By utilizing this information, organizations can customize correspondence, offers, and administrations, cultivating a more grounded association between the client and the brand.

Irregularity across numerous touchpoints is a continuous obstacle in client maintenance endeavors. Customers frequently communicate with businesses via email, social media, and in-person interactions. Guaranteeing a steady and strong experience across these touchpoints is pivotal. Carrying out an omnichannel system that coordinates correspondence and data consistently can assist with overcoming any issues and give a brought together client experience.

Besides, ineffectual correspondence can prompt errors and disappointment. Constantly refreshing clients about new items, advancements, or changes in strategies is fundamental for keeping up with straightforwardness. Clear and compact correspondence helps construct trust and keeps clients informed, diminishing the probability of amazements that could adversely affect their view of the brand.

Client care assumes a critical part in maintenance, and unfortunate client care is a huge hindrance. Customers may leave if there are long wait times, untrained staff, or unresolved issues. The overall customer service experience can be significantly improved by investing in comprehensive training for representatives, streamlining support procedures, and utilizing technology for effective issue resolution.

In the present high speed computerized climate, clients request fast and helpful arrangements. Slow reaction times to questions or deferred issue goal can bring about disappointment. Businesses can increase customer satisfaction by using chatbots, automation, and other technology-driven solutions to provide prompt responses and solutions.

Another test is the absence of a steadfastness program or impetus structure. Clients value being compensated for their dependability, and a very much planned devotion program can fundamentally influence consistency standards. Offering selective limits, early admittance to items, or customized rewards in view of procurement history can boost clients to keep picking a specific brand over contenders.

Cutthroat estimating is a basic calculation of client maintenance. In the event that clients find comparable items or administrations at a lower cost somewhere else, they might be taught to switch suppliers. Leading standard market examinations and changing valuing techniques to stay cutthroat can assist organizations with holding cost delicate clients.

Besides, neglecting to adjust to developing business sector patterns and innovations represents a critical gamble. Embracing development and remaining refreshed on industry progressions is fundamental for staying significant and meeting client assumptions. Organizations that oppose change might end up losing clients to contenders who offer more current and helpful arrangements.

tending to difficulties in client maintenance requires a proactive and all encompassing methodology. From understanding advancing client assumptions to executing customized correspondence and settling issues speedily, organizations should constantly adjust their procedures. By putting resources into innovation, representative preparation, and imaginative arrangements, organizations can conquer normal maintenance difficulties and construct getting through associations with their client base. At last, a client driven outlook and a promise to convey remarkable encounters are principal to effective client maintenance in the present powerful business scene.

Adapting Strategies to Evolving Markets

Adjusting procedures to developing business sectors in client maintenance is a pivotal part of keeping an upper hand in the present unique business scene. As business sectors change, buyer inclinations shift, and advances advance, organizations should be dexterous in their way to deal with holding clients. This article investigates key methodologies for adjusting to developing business sectors and guaranteeing long haul client devotion.

One crucial rule in client maintenance is figuring out the changing requirements and assumptions for your interest group. Statistical surveying assumes a critical part in such a manner, assisting organizations with remaining sensitive to shifts in customer conduct and inclinations. Routinely gathering and breaking down information permits organizations to recognize arising patterns and change their maintenance procedures likewise.

Personalization is one more foundation of effective client maintenance in advancing business sectors. A more engaging and satisfying experience is achieved by tailoring products, services, and communications to individual customer preferences. Utilizing information examination and computerized reasoning can help with grasping client conduct, empowering organizations to convey customized suggestions, offers, and content.

The appearance of advanced innovations has changed the manner in which organizations collaborate with clients. An omnichannel approach is fundamental in adjusting to developing business sectors, as customers progressively expect a consistent encounter across different touchpoints, whether on the web or disconnected. Incorporating client corporations across channels guarantees consistency and upgrades in general consumer loyalty.

In the present quick moving climate, speed is of the substance. Fast reaction to client requests, proficient issue goal, and ideal conveyance of items or administrations contribute essentially to client maintenance. Organizations that focus on responsiveness and dexterity are better situated to meet advancing client assumptions and dominate rivals in unique business sectors.

Building solid associations with clients requires proactive correspondence. Consistently refreshing clients on new contributions, enhancements, or pertinent data keeps them educated as well as supports the association between the brand and the shopper. Utilizing different correspondence channels, including virtual entertainment, email, and informing applications, permits organizations to keep a continuous discourse with their client base.

While obtaining new clients is fundamental for development, it is in many cases more practical to hold existing ones. Unwaveringly projects and motivations can be incredible assets for client maintenance. Offering prizes, limits, or select admittance to steadfast clients empowers rehash business and cultivates a feeling of appreciation.

Imaginative reasoning is basic while adjusting to developing business sectors. Embracing new advancements, investigating novel plans of action, and being available to flighty methodologies can separate a business in a cutthroat scene. Organizations that focus on development are bound to remain in front of market patterns and catch the consideration of knowing customers.

Businesses looking to improve their strategies can benefit greatly from receiving feedback from their customers. Effectively chasing and paying attention to client sentiments gives bits of knowledge into regions to progress and open doors for development. Integrating criticism circles into business processes guarantees a persistent improvement cycle that lines up with developing client assumptions.

When navigating dynamic markets, flexibility is an essential quality for businesses. Being willing to change methodologies, turn when vital, and gain from the two triumphs and disappointments is essential for long haul achievement. Organizations that show flexibility are better prepared to flourish in changing economic situations and fabricate getting through client connections.

Customer retention strategies that work well include employee training and engagement. Forefront staff who are educated, propelled, and compassionate can altogether affect the client experience. Putting resources into continuous preparation projects and encouraging a positive work culture add to representatives' capacity to convey excellent help and construct solid client connections.

adjusting systems to develop business sectors in client maintenance requires an all encompassing and dynamic methodology. From utilizing information examination and personalization to embracing advancement and keeping up with open lines of correspondence, organizations should ceaselessly reconsider and refine their strategies. Those that focus on getting it and meeting the changing requirements of their clients, while staying dexterous and creative, are best situated to flourish in the present steadily advancing business scene.

Chapter 6
Future Trends in Customer Retention

Client maintenance is a basic part of business achievement, and as we plan ahead, a few patterns are molding the manner in which organizations approach and execute procedures to hold their clients. Technology advancements, shifts in consumer behavior, and the ever-evolving business landscape are the driving forces behind these trends.

Personalization at Scale:

One of the noticeable patterns in client maintenance is the expanded spotlight on customized encounters. Companies are using advanced analytics and artificial intelligence to create highly personalized interactions thanks to the abundance of available data. Whether it's fitting item proposals, modifying promoting messages, or offering individualized help, personalization is turning into a vital driver in holding clients.

Man-made intelligence Fueled Client assistance:

Computerized reasoning (man-made intelligence) is changing client care. Chatbots and remote helpers are turning out to be more modern, offering ongoing help and settling issues effectively.

Computer based intelligence calculations examine client connections to recognize designs and foresee expected issues, empowering proactive client support. This improves the client experience as well as adds to consumer loyalty and dedication.

Membership Models and Dependability Projects:

Membership based models and dedication programs are acquiring prominence as successful apparatuses for client maintenance. By offering membership administrations or reliability programs, organizations guarantee a consistent income stream as well as boost clients to remain steadfast. Selective advantages, limits, and customized offers keep clients drew in and persuaded to proceed with their relationship with the brand.

Omni-Channel Commitment:

Today's customers expect a unified experience across all channels. Organizations are coordinating their on the web and disconnected channels to make a firm and predictable brand insight. Whether a client cooperates through virtual entertainment, a portable application, or coming up, the experience ought to be brought together. This omni-channel approach guarantees that clients can progress easily between various touchpoints, cultivating more grounded associations.

Information Protection and Trust:

Customers are becoming more concerned about how their information is handled as a result of the rising incidence of data breaches and privacy concerns. Future-centered client maintenance techniques focus on straightforwardness and proactive measures to safeguard client information. Constructing and keeping up with entrust with clients is fundamental, and organizations that focus on information security and protection will probably see higher standards for dependability.

Proactive Client Commitment:

A growing trend is anticipating customer needs and addressing concerns before they become issues. Using data analytics to identify potential issues and offer solutions before customers even realize there is a problem is proactive customer engagement. In addition to preventing churn, this strategy demonstrates a dedication to customer satisfaction.

Voice of the Client (VoC) Investigation:

In order to improve products and services, it is essential to listen to feedback from customers. VoC investigation includes progressed apparatuses that break down client criticism across different channels, extricating bits of knowledge to upgrade the client experience. By understanding client opinions and inclinations, organizations can settle on information driven choices to tailor their contributions and work on in general fulfillment.

Accentuation on Profound Associations:

Past conditional connections, organizations are perceiving the significance of close to home associations with clients. Brands that inspire positive feelings and reverberate with clients on an individual level are bound to hold them. This includes narrating, making critical encounters, and adjusting brand values to those of the clients.

Prescient Examination for Stir Anticipation:

The ability to identify patterns that indicate potential churn is becoming more sophisticated in predictive analytics. Companies are able to predict which customers are likely to leave by analyzing customer behavior, purchase history, and engagement metrics. Equipped with this data, organizations can carry out designated maintenance procedures to keep important clients.

Social and environmental responsibility:

A developing pattern in client maintenance is the accentuation on ecological and social obligation. Clients are progressively disposed to help marks that exhibit a promise to maintainability and social causes. Organizations incorporating these qualities into their tasks draw in earth and socially cognizant clients as well as encourage long haul unwaveringly.

All in all, the eventual fate of client maintenance is formed by a mix of innovation, client assumptions, and cultural movements. Organizations that embrace personalization, influence computer based intelligence for client care, and focus on trust and straightforwardness are probably going to flourish. The critical lies in understanding the developing necessities of clients and adjusting systems likewise, guaranteeing that client maintenance stays a focal concentration in the powerful scene of business.

Emerging Technologies Impacting Customer Loyalty

Arising advancements are reshaping the scene of client steadfastness in remarkable ways, changing the manner in which organizations draw in and hold their client base. As we delve deeper into the intricate web of these technologies, it becomes clear that they have an impact on a variety of industries. As a result, businesses must adapt or risk falling behind in this digital age that is rapidly changing.

Artificial intelligence (AI) is one prominent technology that influences customer loyalty. Businesses can now personalize customer experiences to an unprecedented degree thanks to cutting-edge algorithms and machine learning. Artificial intelligence breaks down immense measures of client information, permitting organizations to figure out individual inclinations and conduct. This, thus, empowers the conveyance of tailor-made suggestions, advancements, and correspondence, cultivating a feeling of individualized consideration that reinforces client dedication.

Another example of AI that has changed customer interactions is chatbots. These shrewd menial helpers give moment reactions to client inquiries, improving the general client support insight. They are accessible all day, every day, tending to client concerns quickly and proficiently, prompting expanded fulfillment and devotion. The instantaneousness and accommodation they offer contribute essentially to building enduring connections among clients and organizations.

In the field of customer loyalty, blockchain technology is yet another disruptive force. Blockchain ensures the integrity of loyalty programs by offering transactions that are both secure and transparent. Dependency focuses and remunerates, frequently vulnerable to extortion or abuse, can now be safely recorded and checked on a decentralized record. This improves the dependability of devotion programs as well as decreases the probability of debates, subsequently building up client certainty and steadfastness.

The Web of Things (IoT) is consistently incorporating the physical and advanced universes, offering organizations new roads to associate with clients. From connected home appliances to wearable fitness trackers, smart devices produce useful data about user behavior. By utilizing this information, organizations can acquire experiences into client inclinations and propensities, considering the making of customized dedication programs. For example, a wellness application that matches up with a wearable gadget can offer designated rewards in light of the client's work-out daily schedule, cultivating a more grounded connection between the brand and the client.

Increased Reality (AR) and Augmented Reality (VR) advances are rising above conventional limits, empowering vivid and drawing encounters for clients. Retailers, for example, can utilize AR to permit clients to take a stab at items prior to settling on a buy choice essentially. This upgrades the shopping experience as well as adds to a feeling of fulfillment and association, eventually constructing steadfastness towards the brand.

5G innovation is assuming a crucial part in raising client unwaveringly higher than ever. The sped up and network that 5G offers empower consistent and continuous collaborations among clients and organizations. Whether through quicker portable exchanges or improved web-based encounters, the promptness and unwavering quality of 5G add to uplifted consumer loyalty, establishing the groundwork for long haul steadfastness.

Biometric verification is reshaping safety efforts in client collaborations. Biometrics, which include facial and voice recognition, fingerprint recognition, and other biometrics, provide customers with a safe and easy way to access services and conduct business. By incorporating biometric validation into steadfastness programs, organizations can upgrade security and smooth out client encounters, cultivating a feeling of trust and unwavering ness among clients.

Mechanical Cycle Mechanization (RPA) is smoothing out backend activities, permitting organizations to proficiently dispense assets more. This expanded functional effectiveness converts into cost reserve funds, empowering organizations to put more in improving client devotion programs. Customer loyalty is bolstered by dependable and effective service because of RPA's role in process optimization behind the scenes.

Online entertainment stages keep on being powerful in forming client assessments and ways of behaving. Businesses can now understand customer sentiments in real time thanks to emerging social media technologies like predictive analytics and sentiment analysis. Companies are able to tailor their communication strategies by making use of this data, prompting the resolution of issues and bolstering upbeat sentiments to build customer loyalty.

All in all, the effect of arising advancements on client dedication is multi-layered and extraordinary. From artificial intelligence driven personalization to the solid straightforwardness of blockchain, these advances are reshaping the manner in which organizations assemble and keep up with client connections. As organizations explore this scene of development, embracing these advances isn't simply a decision yet a need to remain serious in a market where the client unwaveringly is progressively entwined with the capacity to adjust and use the most recent headways.

Anticipating and Preparing for Market Changes

Expecting and getting ready for market changes in client maintenance procedures is a vital part of keeping an upper hand in the present unique business climate. As business sectors advance and buyer inclinations shift, organizations must proactively adjust their client maintenance systems to remain significant and encourage long haul associations with their customers.

Understanding the constantly changing scene of shopper conduct is the most vital phase in compelling expectation. Directing exhaustive statistical surveying and utilizing information examination can give significant experiences into arising patterns, client inclinations, and potential disruptors. By remaining sensitive to shifts in buyer conduct, organizations can expect changes on the lookout and design their maintenance strategies likewise.

One critical region to zero in on is the computerized scene. Businesses must adapt their customer retention strategies to accommodate the digital preferences of their target audience in light of the growing reliance on online platforms and e-commerce. This incorporates upgrading on the web client encounters, customizing computerized corporations, and utilizing virtual entertainment channels for commitment.

In addition, the ascent of man-made reasoning (artificial intelligence) and AI presents a chance to improve client maintenance methods. Businesses can use these technologies to analyze a lot of customer data to find patterns, predict behavior, and tailor their approach to each customer. This degree of personalization can fundamentally add to consumer loyalty and unwaveringly.

Notwithstanding innovation driven changes, outside variables, for example, financial movements and worldwide occasions can likewise influence client conduct. Organizations should be dexterous in answering these progressions and changing their maintenance procedures as needs be. For example, during financial slumps, offering esteem added administrations, limits, or adaptable installment choices can be viable in holding clients who might be more expense cognizant.

Building a client driven culture inside the association is fundamental for fruitful client maintenance. Workers at all levels ought to be prepared to focus on consumer loyalty and be enabled to instantly determine issues. A client driven approach adds to client devotion as well as upgrades the general standing of the brand.

Expansion of maintenance strategies is one more key component in planning for market changes. Depending on a solitary methodology might become insufficient as customer inclinations develop. Organizations ought to investigate a blend of systems, including unwaveringly programs, customized interchanges, select offers, and magnificent client care, to make an exhaustive maintenance structure.

Client criticism is a priceless asset in expecting and answering business sector changes. Executing hearty input instruments, like studies, surveys, and web-based entertainment observing, can give ongoing experiences into consumer loyalty and regions that need improvement. Effectively paying attention to client criticism empowers organizations to go with informed choices and immediately change their maintenance systems in light of advancing assumptions.

In order to adjust to changes in the market, departments need to work together. Showcasing, deals, client care, and item improvement groups ought to work firmly to adjust their endeavors in conveying a bound together client experience. This cross-useful joint effort guarantees that all parts of the business add to consumer loyalty and maintenance.

Remaining in front of the opposition requires consistent advancement in client maintenance procedures. Organizations ought to consistently survey the viability of their procedures and investigate new ways to deal with draw in clients. Embracing development might include taking on new innovations, exploring different avenues regarding eccentric showcasing strategies, or investigating associations that upgrade the general client experience.

Moreover, expecting market changes includes observing contenders and industry drifts intently. By benchmarking against industry pioneers and dissecting arising patterns, organizations can recognize holes in their maintenance techniques and make proactive changes. Gaining from the triumphs and disappointments of contenders gives important experiences that can illuminate vital choices.

Versatility is a sign of effective organizations despite market changes. A company is better positioned for long-term success if it is able to quickly pivot in response to shifting customer expectations, technological advancements, or external factors. Laying out an adaptable system for client maintenance permits organizations to change their procedures immediately and keep an upper hand on the lookout.

All in all, expecting and planning for market changes in client maintenance methods is fundamental for supported outcome in the present powerful business scene. By remaining informed about arising patterns, utilizing innovation, cultivating a client driven culture, broadening maintenance strategies, gathering and following up on client criticism, advancing cross-useful cooperation, empowering development, observing contenders, and embracing versatility, organizations can proactively explore market changes and fabricate enduring associations with their clients.

CONCLUSION

Customer Retention Techniques and Call to Action for Implementing Strategies

In the consistently developing scene of business, client maintenance remains a significant factor supporting development and productivity. As we investigated different client maintenance strategies all through this conversation, it is clear that a thorough methodology is essential for developing enduring associations with clients. The foundation for successful customer retention is the combination of effective communication, personalized engagement, and proactive strategies.

One pivotal viewpoint we dove into is the significance of understanding client needs and inclinations. By utilizing information examination and client input, organizations can tailor their items and administrations to line up with the assumptions for their customer base. This customized approach encourages client dedication as well as lays out areas of strength for long haul connections.

Another key thought is the job of consistent correspondence in client maintenance. The overall customer experience is enhanced by timely and pertinent communication, whether through individualized interactions or a variety of channels. This approach resolves issues speedily as well as establishes a climate of trust and unwavering quality.

In addition, it is impossible to overstate the significance of employee training in customer-facing positions. Positive interactions with customers are significantly aided by staff members who are knowledgeable and well-equipped. Putting resources into progressing preparing programs guarantees that workers keep up to date with industry drifts and are capable at taking care of client inquiries and concerns successfully.

As we finish up our investigation of client maintenance methods, featuring the arising job of innovation in this landscape is basic. Executing state of the art client relationships the executives (CRM) frameworks, man-made reasoning, and mechanization devices can smooth out processes, permitting organizations to give a more effective and customized client experience.

Source of inspiration: Audit and evaluate Effective

Customer Retention Strategies:

Start by directing an exhaustive review of current client maintenance rehearses. Identify existing strategies' strengths and weaknesses.

Use client criticism and information examination to acquire experiences into client inclinations and conduct.

Personalization Matters:

Foster systems for customized correspondence in light of client information.

Execute customized advertising efforts and advancements.

Utilize CRM systems to efficiently track and utilize customer data.

Preparing and Advancement:

Continuous training for employees who work with customers should be prioritized.

Furnish staff with the information and abilities important for powerful client corporations.

Encourage a client driven culture inside the association.

Influence Innovation:

Put resources into cutting edge CRM frameworks to smooth out client connections.

Investigate the incorporation of computerized reasoning for prescient examination.

Mechanize routine assignments to let loose assets for more customized commitment.

Criticism Instrument:

Lay out a strong criticism system to survey consumer loyalty consistently.

Effectively look for client input on items, administrations, and generally speaking experience.

Use input to repeat and further develop maintenance techniques.

Client Faithfulness Projects:

Plan and execute client devotion projects to boost rehash business.

Offer elite prizes, limits, or early admittance to steadfast clients.

Guarantee straightforwardness and effortlessness in program structures.

Local area Building:

Develop a sensation of the neighborhood in your picture.

Support client commitment through gatherings, web-based entertainment, or elite occasions.

Create a connection that is more than just business.

Adjust and Advance:

Remain receptive to showcase drifts and advancing client assumptions.

Consistently return to and adjust client maintenance methodologies to line up with evolving elements.

Embrace development and test with new methodologies.

All in all, the excursion towards powerful client maintenance is dynamic and requires a comprehensive methodology. By consolidating customized methodologies, embracing innovation, and cultivating a client driven culture, organizations can hold their current client base as well as lay the preparation for manageable development in the cutthroat commercial center. The source of inspiration is clear — coordinate these techniques into your plan of action, adjust them to your interesting setting, and watch as client dedication turns into a foundation of your prosperity.

DEAR READER

Your thoughts matter to us! if the book brought a smile or moment of respite, please Consider Sharing your experience through a review.

Your feedback is invaluable in making our book even more enjoyable to following.We hope this message finds you well and enjoy your literary adventures! We value the opinions of our readers, and we would love to hear your thoughts on **[CUSTOMER RETENTION TECHNIQUES]**.

Thank you for being a part of our literary journey, and we look forward to reading your review!

WARM REGARDS

www.ingramcontent.com/pod-product-compliance
Lightning Source LLC
Chambersburg PA
CBHW071053290526
45795CB00004B/1465